concoctions

concoctions

Recipes for Creeping Crystals, Invisible Ink,
Self-stick Plastic, Grease Paint, Playdough,
and Other Inedibles

Lowi Price and Marilyn Wronsky

E. P. Dutton & Co., Inc.   New York

Library of Congress Cataloging in Publication Data

Price, Lowi   Concoctions

SUMMARY: Recipes, using around-the-house ingredients, for making
a variety of silly and sensible inedible things, such as cosmetics,
inks, pastes, fake plastic, blender paper, and a silver-plated twig.

1. Handicraft—Juvenile literature. [1. Handicraft]
I. Wronsky, Marilyn, joint author. II. Title.
TT160.P8 745.5 76-25842 ISBN 0-525-28137-1

Published simultaneously in Canada by Clarke,
Irwin & Company Limited, Toronto and Vancouver

Editor: Susan Shapiro   Designer: Riki Levinson

Printed in the U.S.A.   First Edition
10 9 8 7 6 5 4 3 2 1

For Peter

Before You Make Concoctions

The concoctions in this book are not for eating. Most of the ingredients and supplies are things you can find around your house. Each recipe makes enough for one or two people.

Some concoctions last for a day or two only. Others last for a long time.

You need a kitchen to work in. Always ask permission to use the kitchen and the ingredients you need.

To make cleanup easy, work on some old newspaper.

If you haven't had practice using a stove, ask for help.

Turn saucepan handles away from the edge of the stove so you won't hit a handle by accident. Some saucepan handles get hot. If yours get hot, use a dry potholder.

When you are finished with the stove, turn off the burner.

A hot saucepan can damage a countertop or table. Set hot pans on a heat-proof surface.

Leave the kitchen clean.

Sometimes a recipe has a sentence written in heavy type. That sentence is a warning. It will look like this:

Don't eat these concoctions. Don't let your sister, or brother, or mother, or father, or best friend, or best enemy, or anybody eat them.

You'll get best results if you follow directions carefully and measure accurately. Use *measuring spoons* and *measuring cups*. This is what the abbreviations mean:

T = Tablespoon
t = teaspoon
c = cup

If you have metric utensils, use these measurements:

for	1 Tablespoon	use	15 ml (milliliter)
	1 teaspoon		5 ml
	1 cup		240 ml
	½ cup		120 ml
	⅓ cup		80 ml
	¼ cup		60 ml

We hope you enjoy making these recipes and that you are pleased with your concoctions.

Lowi and Marilyn

Contents

quick concoctions

Copy Solution

Make prints from comics

1 t vanilla extract
  (or other flavor)
2 t liquid detergent

small dish
2 spoons
  bright-colored comics
  scissors
  white paper
  extra newspaper

Use vanilla, almond, lemon, peppermint, or whatever flavor extract you have. Measure the extract and detergent into a small dish. Stir. This is your copy solution.

Cut out a comic. Lay it face up on some extra newspaper. Cut a piece of white paper a little larger than your comic.

Paint copy solution over the comic with your fingers. Don't miss any spots.

Quickly lay the white paper on the wet comic. Hold it firmly in place. Rub the paper with the back of a dry spoon until the picture shows through.

Lift off your print. You'll have a color copy of the comic. The writing will be backwards.

Silver-plated Twig

You must see it to believe it

wide-mouth jar
water
twig

candle and candleholder
match

Choose a long, dry twig, about as thick as your thumb. **Work outside, away from anything that could burn.** Put a candle firmly into a candleholder. Light it.

Hold onto one end of the twig. Turn the other end slowly in the smoky tip of the flame. Keep the twig moving so it doesn't catch fire. If it does catch fire, blow it out quickly.

Your twig will become evenly and thickly coated with soot. When the soot looks like black velvet, blow out the candle.

Lower the twig into a jar of water. Now you'll see a silver twig.

Dirty Penny Bath

Tarnish remover

2 T vinegar
½ t salt
   cooking oil

saucepan and potholder
spoon
tarnished pennies
paper towel

Measure the vinegar and salt into a saucepan. Stir. Set over medium heat and bring to a boil. Take the pan off the heat and set it on a heat-proof surface. This is your dirty penny bath.

Slide the pennies into the pan. Usually the pennies come clean in an instant. Sometimes you need to stir them around for a minute.

When the tarnish is gone, rinse the pennies in clear water. Dry them well with a paper towel. Damp pennies dull up again.

Your pennies will be clean but not shiny. Put a few drops of oil on a paper towel. Polish the pennies until they gleam.

Don't use your dirty penny bath to clean anything but pennies. Some copper things have a lacquer finish. Dirty penny bath will destroy the lacquer.

Peanut Butter Polish

Works on anything chrome

2 t creamy peanut butter   small dish
2 t baking soda   soft rag

Measure the peanut butter and baking soda into a small dish. Mash together with one finger until you have a smooth ball. This is your peanut butter polish.

You can polish anything chrome. Offer to polish a chrome bumper on a bicycle or car. Brush off the worst of the dirt before you begin. Rub the polish over the bumper. A film will form. Polish with a rag until the bumper shines.

Offer to polish the outside of a toaster or electric coffeepot. Be tidy. Don't get polish in the toaster slots or electric element.

Soap Bubble Mix

For piggyback bubbles

4 drops corn syrup   small dish
1 T liquid detergent   spoon
2 T water   wire coat hanger

Dribble 4 drops of corn syrup into a small dish. Corn syrup is harder to pour than catsup. If you pour too much, spoon the extra back into the bottle.

Add the detergent and water and mix gently. This is your soap bubble mix.

Bend the hook part of a coat hanger to make a bubble loop.

The corn syrup makes the bubbles piggyback. It also makes the mixture slightly sticky.

Use your bubble mix outside.

Creeping Crystals

Don't turn your back

1 T epsom salt
1 T water
¼ t food color
    (any color but yellow)

2 2″ jar lids
saucepan and potholder
spoon

    Measure the epsom salt and water into a saucepan. Cook and stir over medium heat until the salt dissolves. Take the pan off the heat and set on a heat-proof surface. Stir in the food color (yellow doesn't work as well as other colors).

    Pour the mixture into a jar lid. The lid should be almost full. Pour any extra into a second lid.

    Crystals grow as the liquid evaporates. Some form long rods. Some look fine and feathery. Others look like cactus. During the first week they'll creep up and over the lip of the lid.

    Creeping crystals grow slowly for days and last for months.

    You can use liquid creeping crystals as a paint. Brush it on paper, cardboard, or glass. As the liquid dries, frost-like crystals form.

not-so-quick concoctions

Fake Plastic

As tough as the real thing

1 envelope unflavored gelatin	saucepan and potholder spoon
3 T water	plastic coffee-can lid
few drops food color	scissors, paper punch,
(any color you like)	needle, and thread

Measure the gelatin, water, and food color into a saucepan. Cook over medium heat. Stir constantly until all the gelatin grains dissolve. Take the pan off the heat and set it on a heat-proof surface.

Set a plastic lid in an out-of-the-way place. Pour the mixture into the lid. Push any bubbles to the edge. Let the mixture harden for 1 or 2 days.

Lift the gelatin out of the lid when its edges are dry and sharp. Its center should still be rubbery.

Your fake plastic is ready to use. Cut it with scissors to make a ring, a guitar pick, tiddlywinks, and poker chips. To make a sequin necklace, punch out tiny rounds of plastic with a paper punch. String the punchings with a needle and thread.

Let your plastic pieces dry until they're as hard as real plastic. You can thread them and hang them in a sunny window. They'll look like stained glass.

Self-stick Plastic

A sheet of plastic from a puddle of glue

2 t white glue
½ t water
   few drops food color
   (optional)

plastic wrap, 8" square
tape
tray or cookie sheet
small dish
spoon
scissors

Place the plastic wrap on the tray. Smooth it out and tape down the corners. Set the tray flat in an out-of-the-way place.

Mix the glue, water, and food color in a small dish. Pour the mixture onto the center of the plastic wrap. Spread the puddle out evenly. The edges will creep back a bit.

Let the puddle dry. This takes a day or two. The edges may creep back some more. When your plastic is dry, peel it off the plastic wrap. Work carefully. It is very thin and it tears easily.

Self-stick plastic is brittle when cold, but flexible when warm. You can cut it with scissors. You can moisten it with water and stick it to jars, cardboard, or paper. Self-stick plastic will dissolve in water.

Eraser

It really works

1 envelope unflavored gelatin	wax paper, 3″ x 6″
1 T flour	stapler or tape
3 T water	saucepan and potholder
1 T cleansing powder	rubber spatula
	plastic wrap

Fold the wax paper in half so you have a 3-inch square. Fold up the edges of the wax paper to make an eraser-size box. Staple or tape the corners.

Measure the gelatin, flour, and water into a saucepan. Mix with a rubber spatula until smooth. Cook over low heat. Keep scraping the pan with the spatula or you'll lose half your eraser. Cook until very thick, about 5 minutes. Take the pan off the heat and set it on a heat-proof surface. Let the mixture cool a few minutes. Stir in the cleansing powder.

Pour the mixture into the wax paper box. Let it set for several hours. Your eraser is ready to use when it feels dry and rubbery. If it feels damp and cool, it's not ready.

Peel off the wax paper. Try to erase some pencil marks. If the pencil smears, let the eraser dry longer.

Air will make your eraser crispy. To keep it rubbery, wrap it in plastic. After a few days it will mold. Throw it away.

Print Maker

Draw on it and get five prints

1 envelope unflavored
    gelatin
3 T water
½ t liquid detergent

saucepan and potholder
spoon
large lid, metal or plastic
felt-tip pens
white paper (cut into
    small squares)
plastic bag

Measure the gelatin and water into a saucepan. Cook over medium heat. Stir constantly until all the gelatin grains dissolve. Take the pan off the heat and set it on a heat-proof surface.

Stir in the detergent slowly so it doesn't foam.

Pour the mixture into a lid. Push any bubbles to the edge. Let set until the surface is firm, about 3 hours.

Draw a small design on your print maker with felt-tip pens. Write words backward, they'll print forward. Lay a square of paper on your drawing. Rub back and forth across it with your finger. Carefully peel the paper off. If you work quickly, you can make 4 or 5 prints.

This is a self-cleaning print maker. The ink sinks slowly to the bottom and leaves a clean surface. You can draw on your print maker again and again. Store it in a plastic bag. It will keep fresh for about 2 weeks.

Blender Paper

No two papers are ever alike

½ c garden pickings
  (dandelion fluff, grass
  clippings, etc.)
½ c paper (towels, tissue,
  or newspaper)
  water

an adult
blender
wire screen, 10″ square
newspaper
wax paper
rolling pin

Find garden pickings that are tender enough to tear. Tear the pickings and paper into very tiny bits. Measure and put them in the blender. Add water until the blender is half full. Cover the blender.

Ask an adult to operate the blender.

He or she should blend the mixture for 2 minutes or until it looks like confetti soup. Turn off the blender.

Work over the sink. Slowly pour the liquid through the wire screen. The pulp will stay on the screen. Save it.

Place the screen on newspaper. Push and pat the pulp with your fingers to fill in any holes. Cut a piece of wax paper as large as the screen. Lay it over the pulp. Roll lightly with the rolling pin. This will flatten the pulp and squeeze out some of the water.

Put the screen on dry newspaper and roll again. This time roll hard. Change to a dry sheet of newspaper and roll. Do this several times until the newspaper remains dry. Set the screen on newspaper in an out-of-the-way place. Your blender paper will dry in a day.

Peel off the wax paper and lift your blender paper from the screen. The color and texture of your paper depend on the ingredients you use. Its thickness depends on how hard you roll it out.

Sidewalk Chalk

Made from eggshells

6 eggshells (saved from   clean, smooth rock
  eggs you've eaten)   2 small dishes
1 t flour   spoon
1 t very hot tap water   strip of paper towel

Wash and dry the eggshells. Grind them outdoors on clean, smooth concrete with a clean, smooth rock. Grind and grind until you get fine eggshell powder. Sweep it up with your hands and put it into a dish. Pick out any big pieces of eggshell and throw them away.

Measure the flour and hot water into another dish. Stir until you get a paste. Add 1 Tablespoon of the eggshell powder. Mix and mash until it all sticks together.

Shape and press the mixture firmly into a chalk stick. Roll it up tight in the strip of paper towel. Let it dry for 3 days. Your sidewalk chalk will get rock hard.

Tear the paper off one end. Write with the chalk, erase with your shoe.

Sidewalk chalk is for sidewalks, not blackboards.

gussy up

Marshmallow Soap

It floats

1 c soapflakes
½ c water
   few drops food color
     (optional)

milk carton
stapler
wax paper
heavy bowl
saucepan and potholder
rubber spatula
eggbeater

Cut the milk carton into 1-inch strips. Bend the strips into shapes such as hearts, pears, and diamonds. Staple the ends together.

These are forms for drying the soap. Set the forms on wax paper.

Measure the soapflakes into a heavy bowl. Boil the water and pour it over the soap. Stir with a rubber spatula until the soapflakes dissolve completely.

Have a friend hold down the bowl. Beat the mixture with an eggbeater. This is hard work! The soap will get satiny, like taffy. Stir in food color if you want colored soaps.

Fill the milk-carton forms with whipped soap. Smooth off the tops. Let your marshmallow soaps dry for a day. Then pop them out of their forms.

Lipstick

Smells like cocoa, feels like butter

1 t cocoa butter
¼ t cornstarch
few drops red
vegetable color

aluminum foil, 3″ square
fat pencil or felt-tip pen
saucepan and potholder
spoon
small drinking glass
small funnel

You can buy a bar of cocoa butter in a drugstore. It looks like white chocolate.

Wrap the foil around the blunt end of a pencil. Twist one end of the foil closed. Slip it off the pencil. This is your lipstick mold.

Break off a chunk of cocoa butter just big enough to fill a measuring teaspoon. Put it into a saucepan and melt it over low heat. Take the pan off the heat and set it on a heat-proof surface. Measure the cornstarch into the pan. Stir until the mixture is absolutely smooth. Add vegetable color until you get a shade you like.

Prop the foil mold in a small glass. Use a funnel to pour the liquid lipstick into the mold. Set the lipstick in the refrigerator for 10 minutes to cool and harden.

Peel the foil from the open end of your lipstick. Round the top with your fingers. It's ready to use. Keep your lipstick cool. Cocoa butter melts at body temperature.

Oatmeal Face Mask

Shrinks to fit

1 T quick-cooking oats   small dish
1 T very hot tap water   spoon
                                  pillow
                                  soft towel

Measure the oatmeal and hot water into a small dish. Stir until you have a smooth oatmeal paste.

If you have long hair, tie it back. Spread the paste on your face with your fingertips. Spread up from your chin, your face will dry into a smile. Spread down from your forehead, your face will frown.

Keep the paste away from your eyes, lips, and hair.

The mask should dry as slowly as possible. Find a cool, quiet place to lie down. Prop your feet up on a pillow.

Let the mask dry for 10 minutes. You'll feel it get stiff and tight. If you talk or laugh, you'll get pinched.

Wash the mask off with warm water. Pat your face dry with a towel. Your face will tingle.

Hand Lotion

Cool as a cucumber

½ cucumber
  few drops lemon
    extract

medium-size bowl
soft cloth or
  handkerchief
grater
spoon
tiny jar with lid

    Line a medium-size bowl with a soft cloth. The edges of the cloth should hang over the rim of the bowl.

    Wash the cucumber. Grate it onto the cloth.

    Gather up the corners of the cloth. Twist the cloth so the cucumber pulp is pressed into a ball. Wring and squeeze as much juice as you can into the bowl. Throw away the pulp.

    Stir a few drops of lemon extract into the cucumber juice.

    Spoon your hand lotion into a tiny jar. Try it. It feels cool and not even sticky. Keep the jar covered and in the refrigerator. Your lotion will stay fresh for a few days.

Perfume

Good scents

1 c fragrant flower petals
1 c water

medium-size bowl
soft cloth
saucepan and potholder
small funnel
tiny jar with lid

Ask permission to gather sweet-smelling petals, such as roses, lilacs, or violets.

Line a medium-size bowl with a soft cloth. The edges of the cloth should hang over the rim of the bowl. Tear the petals into bits. Measure them and drop them onto the cloth.

Boil the water in a saucepan and pour it over the petals. Make sure all the petals are covered with water. Let them soak overnight.

The next day, gather up the corners of the petal-filled cloth. Lift the cloth out of the water and hold it over the bowl. Wring and squeeze the water from the petals. Throw them away. Put the scented water into a pan. Simmer it until just 1 teaspoonful is left. Let cool.

Use a funnel to pour your perfume into a jar. Use a dab of it. Keep the jar covered. Your perfume will stay fresh for about a month.

Bath Salts

Blue bath salts won't turn you blue

¼ c epsom salt
7 drops food color
   (any color you like)

large jar with
   screw-top lid
small jar with lid

Measure the epsom salt and food color into a large jar. Screw the lid on tight. Shake the jar to spread the color.

Pour your bath salts into a small jar.

When you take a bath, add a big pinch of salts to the water.

Bath salts may make the tub slippery. Be careful.

Green bath salts won't turn you green. Orange bath salts won't turn you orange. Purple bath salts won't. . . .

Make two different colors of bath salts and layer them in your prettiest jar as a gift for a friend.

ink

Iron Ink

Turn tea into ink

1 tea bag
¼ c water
1 old scouring pad

clean tin can
saucepan and potholder
small jar with
   screw-top lid
toothpick and writing
   paper

The scouring pad must be steel (gray). Copper and plastic pads won't work. Wash all the soap out of the pad. Squeeze it dry.

Measure the water into a saucepan. Bring it to a boil.

Put a tea bag in a tin can. Add the boiling water and wait 10 minutes. Lift out the tea bag and squeeze all the tea into the can. The tea should be *very strong*.

Drop the scouring pad into the tea. The tea will turn black instantly. Let the pad soak in the tea overnight.

Lift out the pad. Set a small jar in the sink and pour your iron ink into it.

Iron ink stains, so don't spill it.

Write with a toothpick.

Iron ink keeps 3 or 4 days in a covered jar. When it begins to smell and mold, throw it out.

Lampblack Ink

Write with soot

¼ t lampblack
¼ t white glue
4 drops water

candle and candleholder
old tablespoon
jar lid
toothpick and writing
paper

Work outdoors, away from anything that could burn.
Set a candle firmly in a candleholder. Light it. Hold a tablespoon upside down over the smoky tip of the flame.

Soot, or lampblack, will begin to coat the inside of the spoon. Collect lampblack for at least 20 minutes. It should be very thick on the spoon.

Blow out the candle.

Scrape the lampblack out of the spoon and measure it into a jar lid. Add the glue and water. Mix and mash with the back of the lampblack spoon until you get a smooth ink. This takes time.

Write with a toothpick. Lampblack ink dries with a hard, shiny finish.

Invisible Ink

Now you don't see it, now you do

4 drops onion juice
4 drops lemon juice
17 grains sugar
   (count them)

knife
small jar lid
toothpick and writing
   paper
light bulb

Slice a piece off the end of the onion and the lemon. Squeeze out the juice you need. Mix the onion juice, lemon juice, and sugar in a jar lid. Stir with a toothpick until the 17 grains of sugar are dissolved.

Write with the toothpick. If you press too hard, grooves will show in the paper and give away your message.

Let the ink dry. Your message will disappear.

Invisible ink becomes visible when heated. Hold the paper over a bright light bulb.

Your message will reappear in brown letters.

Salt Writing

Another invisible ink

½ t salt
½ t hot water

small jar lid
toothpick and writing
    paper
soft pencil

Measure the salt and hot water into a jar lid. Stir with a toothpick until most of the salt dissolves. This is your ink.

Use the toothpick to write. Make your letters large. If you press too hard, grooves will show in the paper and give away your message.

Salt writing is visible while it's wet. Let it dry for 30 minutes. Your message will be invisible.

To make your message reappear, rub across the paper with pencil lead. The lead blackens the dried salt more than it blackens the paper. Your message appears in black writing as the paper turns gray.

Watermarking

An invisible ink with no ingredients

2 sheets of paper
pan of water
tray
pencil or ball-point pen

Dip 1 sheet of paper into a pan of water. Lift it out and let it drip over the pan. Spread it out smooth on a tray or countertop. Cover it with the dry sheet of paper.

Hold the 2 sheets of paper firmly in place. Write your message on the top sheet. Press hard. Lift the top sheet off. Your words will be imprinted on the bottom sheet.

Destroy the top sheet of paper so there will be no copy of your message. Let the bottom sheet dry. Your message will vanish.

To make the writing reappear, dip the paper in water again.

You can make the writing appear and disappear as many times as you want. The message is visible when the paper is wet. It's invisible when the paper is dry.

paint and dye

Grease Paint

Paint-yourself-up paint

1 t cornstarch
½ t water
½ t cold cream
    few drops food color
        (any color you like)

small dish
spoon
tiny jar with lid

Measure the cornstarch and water into a small dish. Mix until smooth. Stir in the cold cream. Add the food color a drop at a time. Stop when you get a color you like.

If you have long hair, tie it back.

Put your grease paint on thick.

Keep it away from your eyes.

It works best where you don't wrinkle.

Grease paint washes off with soap and water.

Air will dry out your grease paint. Keep any extra paint covered in a tiny jar.

Fingerpaint

Like painting with pudding

1 T cornstarch
1 T soapflakes
4 T water
1 t hand lotion
   few drops food color
     (any color you like)

saucepan and potholder
rubber spatula
paper or cardboard
jar with lid

Measure the cornstarch, soapflakes, and water into a saucepan. Mix well with a rubber spatula.

Cook over medium heat. The mixture will be milky at first. Stir constantly with the spatula until it foams and thickens. The soapflakes will dissolve. Take the pan off the heat and set it on a heat-proof surface.

Stir in the hand lotion. Add food color a drop at a time until you get a color you like. Let cool.

Use your fingerpaint on paper or cardboard. It's like painting with creamy pudding.

If you have paint left over, keep it tightly covered in a jar. It will stay fresh for months.

Speedy Dye

No-cook dye for hard-cooked eggs

2 T vinegar
 few drops food color
  (any color you like)

small dish
hard-cooked egg
spoon
newspaper
cake rack

Measure the vinegar into a small dish. Stir in food color a drop at a time. You can mix a new color from two colors. Stop when you get a color you like.

Slide the egg into the dish. Roll it around and spoon dye over it. Speedy dye works in seconds. For a darker color, leave the egg in longer.

Vinegar attacks eggshell. If you want a speckled egg, let it sit in the dye about 20 minutes. Keep spooning dye over it.

Put newspaper under a cake rack to catch drips. Put your egg on the rack to dry. Don't rinse it. Water will wash speedy dye off the egg.

Keep your egg in the refrigerator until you eat it.

Onion Skin Dye

Gold, orange, or reddish-brown

1 c onion skins
   (yellow or red)
2 c water

saucepan with lid
potholder
spoon
newspaper
all-cotton cloth or string

Use skins from yellow or red onions. White skins won't work.

Measure the onion skins and water into a saucepan. Stir. Cover the pan. Cook over medium heat until the dye starts to simmer. Simmer 20 minutes. Take the pan off the heat and set it on newspaper on a heat-proof surface.

Onion skin dye stains, so work carefully.

You can leave the onion skins in the dye. Push the cloth into the dye. Stir until it is completely wet. Be sure no peaks of cloth stick above the surface of the dye. Cover the pan.

In an hour your cloth will be gold, orange, or reddish-brown. If you let it sit in the dye bath overnight, it will be more colorfast.

In the morning, squeeze the dye out of your cloth and rinse it in a small amount of water. Hang it in the shade to dry. Your cloth won't be completely colorfast. When it needs washing, rinse it quickly in cold water.

Red Cabbage Blue

Denim-blue dye

1 c red cabbage choppings
1 c water
1 T salt

knife and chopping
  board
iron cooking pot with lid
potholder
spoon
newspaper
all-cotton cloth or string

Chop the red cabbage into small pieces. Measure the cabbage and water into an iron pot. The water will start to turn blue. (This dye works best in an iron pot. If you don't have one, use an old saucepan.)

Sprinkle the salt over the cabbage and water. The salt turns blue instantly. Stir until the salt dissolves.

Cover the pot and cook over medium heat until the dye starts to simmer. Simmer 10 minutes. Take the pan off the heat and set it on newspaper on a heat-proof surface.

Red cabbage dye stains, so work carefully.

Push the cloth into the dye. Stir until it is completely wet. Be sure no peaks of cloth stick above the surface of the dye. Cover the pan. Let the cloth sit in the dye overnight.

In the morning, squeeze the dye out of your cloth and rinse it in a small amount of water. Hang it in the shade to dry. Your cloth won't be completely colorfast. When it needs washing, rinse it quickly in cold water.

paste and glue

Quick Paste

For paper or papier-mâché

1 T flour
1 T cold water
2 T boiling water

small dish
spoon
saucepan and potholder
small jar

Measure the flour and the cold water into a small dish. Stir until smooth.

Boil the 2 Tablespoons of water. Pour it over the flour mixture. Stir until smooth. The paste will be thin. Spoon your quick paste into a small jar. Let cool a few minutes before you try to use it.

Quick paste keeps for 2 or 3 days. Leave the jar uncovered. If it separates, stir it. When it begins to smell yeasty, throw it out.

Thick Paste

Add alum to keep it fresh

1 t sugar
1 T flour
¼ t powdered alum
   (optional)
4 T water

saucepan and potholder
rubber spatula
small jar with
   screw-top lid

Measure the sugar and flour into a saucepan. If you add alum, it will keep the paste from spoiling. Add 1 Tablespoon of the water and stir with a rubber spatula until smooth. Add the rest of the water and mix well.

Cook over medium heat, stirring constantly. Keep scraping the bottom and sides of the pan. Paste burns easily. Cook until thick and smooth.

Spoon the paste into a jar. Let cool a few minutes before you try to use it.

Thick paste with alum will stay fresh for 2 weeks. Keep the jar tightly covered. When mold starts to form on the top, throw it out.

Strawberry Stamps

Tasty stickum

1 t strawberry gelatin   slick magazine
  (or other flavor)   scissors
2 t water   newspaper
                    saucepan and potholder
                    spoon

Make stamps and decals by cutting colored pictures from a slick magazine. Lay them face down on newspaper.

Measure the gelatin and water into a saucepan. Bring to a boil over medium heat. Stir constantly until all the gelatin grains dissolve. Take the pan off the heat and set on a heat-proof surface. Let cool a minute.

Work while the stickum is still warm. Paint an even coat on the back of each stamp with your finger. Let your strawberry stamps dry for 1 or 2 days. They may curl as they dry.

When they're dry, lick them and stick them to stationery, envelopes, greeting cards, and glass jars.

Gelatin Glue

Nice warm glue

1 envelope unflavored
    gelatin
3 T water

saucepan and potholder
spoon

Measure the water into a saucepan. Add the gelatin. Stir until mixed.

Cook over medium heat. Stir constantly until all the gelatin grains dissolve. Take the pan off the heat and set it on a heat-proof surface.

Let your glue cool enough so you can touch it. Use it while it's still warm. It gels at room temperature. If your glue thickens before you are finished with it, set the glue pan in a larger pan of hot water. The glue will melt again.

Use gelatin glue for paper and cardboard. It dries smooth and clear.

Glue Factory Glue

Make gelatin glue from scratch

bones from 1 cooked chicken
water

saucepan with lid
potholder
large spoon
strainer
small dish

Break the smaller bones into pieces. Put all the bones and pieces in a saucepan. Add enough water to cover the bones completely.

Put the lid on the pan. Cook over medium heat until the water starts to simmer. Turn the heat to low and simmer 1 hour. Check every 15 minutes to make sure the water still covers the bones. Add more water if necessary.

Take the lid off the pan. Turn the heat to high. Boil the water until only 1 Tablespoon is left.

Watch constantly while you do this, so the pan doesn't boil dry.

Take the pan off the heat and set on a heat-proof surface.

Let cool a few minutes. Push all the bones together with a spoon, and lift as many as you can out of the pan. Throw them away.

The liquid that's left is your glue factory glue. Pour it through a strainer into a dish. Use it while it is warm. It will gel as it cools.

Milk Glue

Turn sour milk into glue

¼ c nonfat milk
½ t vinegar
½ t baking soda
1 T warm water

saucepan and potholder
spoon
strainer
2 small dishes

Measure the milk into a saucepan. Warm it over low heat. Take the pan off the burner as soon as steam begins to rise. Set the pan on a heat-proof surface.

Stir in the vinegar. Keep stirring until the milk separates into curds and whey. Strain off the liquid whey. Save the white curd.

Measure the baking soda and warm water into a small dish. Mash the curd into the soda-water. This will be foamy and lumpy.

Press this mixture through a strainer into a clean dish. Now it will be grainy. Set it aside for a day. The grains of curd will dissolve.

Your milk glue is ready when it turns smooth and clear.

clay, dough,
and carving stone

Bread Heads

Pumpernickel, whole wheat, rye, or white

2 slices very soft bread,   breadboard
   without seeds   knife
1 t white glue
2 t water
   few drops food color
   egg white (optional)

Place the bread on a board and use a knife to trim off the crusts. Smear the slices with glue and sprinkle with water.

Knead the bread until it is absolutely smooth. This takes time. If it gets dry, knead in a little more water.

Take a marble-sized piece of bread-clay and flatten it into a face. Knead food color into bits of clay for eyes, lips, and hair. Moisten these bits and stick them on the face. Make the bread heads small so they'll dry without cracking.

Let your bread heads dry for a day. For a satiny finish, shellac them with egg white.

Toothpaste Putty
It's stretchy

½ t toothpaste (creamy kind)
1 t white glue
2 t cornstarch
¼ t water

small dish
powdered pencil lead
  (optional)

Use creamy toothpaste. Jelly-like toothpastes don't work. Measure the toothpaste, white glue, and corn-starch into a small dish. Mix well with one finger. It will be crumbly.

Add the water. Mix and mix until you have a lump of putty. The lump should clean the dish. If it doesn't, add a drop of water and keep mixing. Wash and dry your hands. Squeeze and roll your toothpaste putty into a smooth ball. The more you roll it the better it gets. Make a worm. Push it and pull it. Toothpaste putty is elastic.

Your putty will begin to dry in about 20 minutes. If you want to keep working with it, soften it with a drop of water.

Toothpaste putty can also make a rock. Scrape lead from a pencil point with a small knife. Roll your putty in the powdered pencil lead until it looks like granite. If you roll it for too long you'll get a black boulder. Let your rock dry for a day. It will get rock hard.

Soap Stone

Bright-colored carving stone

4 T very finely chopped
    hand soap
	knife
	old saucepan and
	    potholder

3 T water	
2 T very finely chopped crayon	old spoon wax paper

Measure the soap choppings and water into a saucepan. Set over low heat.

If your soap is perfumed, open a window.

Cook and stir until the soap is melted and the water is gone. The mixture should be thick and satiny.

Add the crayon choppings. Cook and stir until they melt completely. Scrape the mixture out onto wax paper. Let it cool until you can touch it.

Clean your pan and spoon right away.

Once this mixture cools it is difficult to clean off.

Press the mixture firmly into 2 or 3 stones. The surface will be rough. Let dry for 1 or 2 days.

Carve your soap stone with a small knife. You can make richly colored wax animals, jewels, chess pieces, and many other shapes.

Playdough

Use it over and over and over

½ c flour   medium-size bowl
2 T salt   saucepan and potholder
1 t cream of tartar   spoon
  (optional)   jar with lid
⅓ c water
1 t cooking oil

Measure the flour and salt into a bowl. Add cream of tartar if you want your playdough to last a long time. Boil the water in a saucepan and pour it into the flour mixture. Add the oil. Stir until the dough is well mixed and you can push it into a lump. It will be sticky.

Pick up the ball of warm dough. Roll and squeeze it between your hands until the stickiness disappears. Knead it for 5 minutes. The longer you handle it, the nicer it gets. It's ready to use when it makes a smooth, elastic ball.

You can use your playdough over and over. Store it in a tightly covered jar.